EMBRACE THE RIDICULOUSNESS

A POCKET GUIDE TO BEING A BETTER YOU

BY JEN COKEN

Embrace the Ridiculousness: A Pocket Guide to Being A Better You
Copyright © 2018 by Jen Coken

Published by Myril Press
ISBNs:
978-1-7326286-0-1 (trade paperback)
978-1-7326286-1-8 (Kindle ebook)
978-1-7326286-2-5 (epub ebook)

Printed in the United States of America
Designed and Illustrated by 0melapics / Freepik
Edited by Mary Ann Tate, The Art of Words

www.jencoken.com

This book is dedicated to Erica Breuer, for her vision, creativity, and general all-around badassery. You are one gifted human being. This book would not have gotten done without you!

With all my love and respect, Jen

WHAT THIS BOOK
IS ALL ABOUT

I HAVE COACHED THOUSANDS OF PEOPLE over the last 20 years. From Members of Congress, CEO's, and Executive Directors of Nonprofits to entrepreneurs and college students. There is one thing these people have in common: they are already successful but secretly dissatisfied with some aspect of their lives.

It may be that they feel they haven't quite achieved the real success they want. They might be overwhelmed with what is on their plate. They may want more from their relationships and the way they spend their precious hours.

No matter who they are, they always want to know how to deal with life's challenges with a smile on their faces.

Whether you're highly successful and secretly unsatisfied, juggling a tangle of responsibilities, or wading your way through a full-stop crisis, this book will help you. It will show you how to look at the hard stuff, laugh at life's absurdity, and raise the bar on yourself.

I wrote this book because I live for helping people achieve breakthroughs. We're here to fulfill a destiny, after all!

Achieving your goals is one thing. Shirking old have-to's and should haves is another.

But, are you able to go beyond what you think you're capable of? That's what this book revolves around.

Each chapter gives short, no-nonsense how-to's to get you going, combined with "pondering questions" and exercises that will help you level up your skills and retrain old habits.

With some passion, attention, resilience, and a sense of humor, you can start living your best life now. You can achieve the things you've always dreamed of, and stress less. You'll form the connections you've always wanted and have plenty of time for the things you love (even when the "s**t" hits the fan).

And you'll embrace life's ridiculousness along the way.

So, what are you waiting for? Turn the page and sink your teeth into Chapter One like it's a Nutella-filled crepe!

With Gratitude,
Jen

TABLE OF CONTENTS

CHAPTER ONE

DON'T SET SMART GOALS — THEY'RE STUPID

A S A MANAGER, GRASSROOTS ORGANIZER, and life coach for the last 20 years, I've talked to and worked with a lot of people. Through those experiences, I've concluded that there are five common mistakes unsuccessful people make. The first one I'll take about in this chapter is that they get hung up on making "S.M.A.R.T." goals in every area of life. You may recall that the term S.M.A.R.T. stands for specific, measurable, achievable, realistic, and time- based.

This term was created to ensure that project managers and others got their work done. "Plan your work and work your plan" is a common phrase you hear in many industries. So S.M.A.R.T. goals are designed to ensure that you succeed, which makes sense, right? Why, oh why, would anyone set themselves up for failure?

I say S.M.A.R.T. goals are stupid because applying this technique to your personal life or personal achievement of a big dream actually inhibits you.

Creating S.M.A.R.T. goals stop you from dreaming big, thinking creatively, and playing full out. If you know you can achieve your goals, how much ingenuity does it take? How much are you going to go outside of your comfort zone? Probably not a lot, and that's

---

why unsuccessful people find themselves bored and frustrated with life. Their goals are small. If they achieve them without much effort, there is little experience of success. If they don't achieve them, they start thinking of themselves as someone who is unable to produce the results they want.

On the flip side, successful people set big, hairy, audacious goals—goals that will be worthy of their time and worthy of the possibility of failure. Successful people put their butts on the line for something big because playing out there on the skinny branches of life is exhilarating—it's where our creative juices begin to flow. It's where ideas are hatched and connections are made. Successful people get a lot of juice out of playing full out even if they fail, because they take the time to reflect and understand where they grew and developed.

When I speak to my clients they often focus on the negative consequences when they do not achieve a goal. I shouldn't be surprised because 80% of our thoughts are negative according to a University of Michigan study. We often do a "post mortem" when we've failed, but do we ever dissect our work to figure out what made us succeed? Not very often.

The good news: in only fifteen minutes and by answering only ten simple questions, you can start thinking and acting like a successful person by reviewing and celebrating your wins. Once you answer these questions you will begin to get a handle on what made you successful and be able to repeat or expand those strategies. This is what I call people finding their own "secret success sauce".

Questions to Ask Yourself:

1. What were your biggest achievements this year? These are the big ones, the medium-sized ones, and the small ones. Don't skimp here!

2. What are the biggest challenges you overcame?

3. What did you learn about yourself? Did you identi
new strengths, weaknesses, goals, talents, skills, or abilities?

4. Where did you grow or develop new skills toward achieving your larger goals? (It is important to recognize the places you grew and developed as you worked toward achieving those larger goals, even if you didn't achieve them.)

5. What did you achieve that surprised you?

6. What did you fail at, or make a mistake with that needs recognizing? FYI: Successful people know that failing does not make them a failure. They know that success itself is marked by a whole lot of wins and a whole lot of losses. Not recognizing failure could cause you to repeat the same mistakes or overlook a pattern. Take some time to recognize your failures with a compassionate eye.

7. What new habits did you develop this year? These could be good habits you developed, or bad habits that you want to acknowledge and not carry over into the new year.

8. What new relationships did you build or develop?

9. What did you enjoy the most of your life this year? Where did you have fun, even when things were tough??

Our success can come in many forms. It can come from the obstacles we overcame, the relationships we built, or even how much fun we had! Shut the front door! Not fun, Jen? YES! Having fun while you are in the middle of something stressful is a GREAT accomplishment.

10. What will you do to celebrate, recognize, and acknowledge your achievements? Write down what you are going to do to celebrate, with whom, and when. Whether it is seeing a friend, getting a massage, going out to dinner. It's important to recognize your success!

And one last note about successful people: When they walk through this exercise, they identify achievement gaps. From there, they set out to connect with others who can help them close those achievement gaps—if you'd like to learn more about how I do this personally, skip to the last chapter entitled, "Make A Huge Investment (This Is NOT Stock Advice!)."

CHAPTER TWO

SHUT. YOUR. INNER CRITIC. UP.

MRS. LEFFERTS WAS ONE OF my high school English teachers. She was a towering woman, about six feet tall. She wore long skirts, white blouses that were too small, and dark brown, thick-soled men's shoes. You could tell her bras were ill-fitting too, because she was constantly reaching in and adjusting the straps when she thought we weren't looking.

Mrs. Lefferts was also a total pain in my butt. She was constantly on my case to pay more attention in class. She wanted me to succeed, to improve my writing skills, and think more critically as I drafted outlines for my papers. See, in high school I was what you would call a slacker. I used to cut class and go smoke cigarettes in the courtyard, or hang out at Arthur Treacher's Fish and Chips with my friends. One year, I missed a total of one hundred and twenty-nine classes. I remember because when I showed my report card to my mom, I lied and told her the system was flawed.

"Everyone's report cards have problems, Mom!" But she never believed me. She just had a repairman come out and turn off the TV for the summer. I was left to read a lot of books and live with my lies. By the way, I never suspected that she knew a thing until she confessed 10 years later!

Today I owe Mrs. Lefferts an apology for making fun of her behind her back, as well as a huge debt of gratitude. Her class made all the difference for me in college. I wouldn't have achieved so many A's on my papers without her guidance (Thanks, Mrs. Lefferts, wherever you are).

While her feedback and scrutiny made me the writer I am today, I can still hear her shrill voice in my head. I'm sure she was giving me constructive criticism back then. But, unfortunately, that voice still rings in my ears as the voice of my inner critic. That critic pops up at the most inopportune times.

My inner critic is constantly telling me that I need to do more, produce more, apply myself more, be more serious, take on more —more, more, more, more, more! As a friend once said to me, "You get more done before breakfast than most people do in a day."

She's actually right, but my inner critic only notices what I haven't done and never, ever, lets me celebrate what I have accomplished.

Acknowledging our inner critic is a very powerful tool. It brings a greater awareness to the critical or judging element within us—t hat then gives us the opportunity to make changes and do things differently.

One way of looking at your inner critic or judge is to see it as a habitual way of thinking. When you were small, that critic helped you stay out of trouble. It protected you by repeating what it saw and heard from authority figures—teaching you how to stay safe by doing well, and avoiding displeasing those who were crucial to your survival. But while you have grown up and moved on, your inner critic has not. It still bullies, judges and criticizes you to keep you safe!

Your inner critic dates back to when adults knew best, when they were right, and children were wrong. This is how your critic views the world. But you are no longer a child, you have your OWN values, beliefs, and ways of doing things. You and can think for,

Jen Coken

decide for, and protect yourself. You don't have to please others to survive.

To identify and acknowledge your inner critic, walk through this simple visualization:

1. Close your eyes and get present to a moment when you could hear your inner critic. It might have been as soon as your feet hit the floor this morning, or the moment things weren't going quite the way you planned.

2. Get present to the energy of that moment: What did it feel like in your body? Was your energy level low or high? What were your emotions?

3. Put yourself right back in those moments when you could hear your inner critic loud and clear. What does your inner critic sound and look like? Who does your inner critic remind you of?

4. Picture your inner critic in your mind's eye. What does he or she look like? Draw it out!

When I walked through this visualization, I spent forty-eight hours intently listening for what my inner critic was saying to me in preparation for a workshop I was leading.

I then got to work and drew a picture of my inner critic. There she was with her arms crossed, foot impatiently tapping, looking over the top of her glasses at me with her ill-fitting blouse. MRS. LEFFERTS! I may have needed her in high school to egg me on (and thank goodness she did), but as a successful adult with my OWN values, beliefs, and ways of doing things, I don't need her to motivate me anymore.

Once I realized this, I created a power statement. A "power statement" is a simple statement starting with "I am" that gives you energy and makes you feel empowered.

I created: "I am a go-getter!" Every time my inner critic tells me to do more, I tell it to shut up, and remind myself that I am a go-getter. When I share that with others, it makes me realize (again) that I do get a lot done, and I don't have to listen to that voice in my head.

Who is your inner critic? What does it say to you? When does it get triggered? If you weren't listening to your inner critic what would you do with that time? What would your power statement be?

CHAPTER THREE

JUST BE YOU, YOU'RE ENOUGH

THIS IS YET ANOTHER CHAPTER dedicated to the negative thoughts and chatter that exist between our ears. I did this BECAUSE THAT CRITIC IN OUR HEADS NEVER SHUTS UP. Just pause for a second...what is that voice commenting on right now? It could be the weather, the shampoo you used this morning, how uncomfortable your chair is. Or maybe you are thinking, "what voice in my head?"

That voice is exactly what I'm pointing out to you. That voice tells you what is right and wrong with you, everyone else, and everything else around you. All you have to do is commute in rush hour traffic, and you'll hear its running commentary if you don't believe me.

Overcoming negative self-talk and inner critics make up a huge amount of the work I do with my clients. Everyone has voices that go unchecked and 80% of the time the thoughts are negative. I want you, dear reader, to have options when it comes to tackling this stuff—because the solutions to changing these habits aren't exactly one-size-fits-all. I'm also giving you ample time to absorb this topic, because it's one I've struggled with in different shapes and forms time and again.

In fact, I used to be the queen of making negative comments about myself. Kind of a weird thing, given I'd been coaching other people to stop doing that for years.

But you don't always realize what you are saying to yourself until someone else you are living with hears you and addresses it. Picture me, standing in front of my full-length mirror after getting dressed, smoothing out my hips attempting to straighten the curves I'd been born with and had never been proud of. My then-husband caught me doing this one day and asked me what I was doing.

"I just wish my thighs were smaller and my hips weren't so big," I whined.

"First, women are supposed to be curvy," he said, "Second, stop talking smack about my best friend Jen."

His reply stopped me dead in my tracks. No one had ever said that, in that way, to me before.

Whether it is complaining about the way we look, calling ourselves stupid or silly, or comparing ourselves to someone else and coming up short—we say things to ourselves we'd never dare to say to a good friend.

Unfortunately, most of us do this on some level.

Take for instance, my client "Tammy". I've known Tammy for at least 10 years. Tammy grew up with a mother who she experienced as highly critical, so she learned to please her.

She did what she was told, which mostly included making herself quieter, smaller, and unobtrusive so that her mother could shine.

Unfortunately, Tammy didn't just apply that learned behavior to her relationship with her mother. As she grew up, she applied that behavior to every relationship. She had learned from her mom that if she outshined someone she loved, they would take their love away. So, that learned behavior just became part of her identity—of who she knew herself to be. "I'm just shy," she would say. Gentle internal smack talking...but still smack talking.

Every time you criticize yourself you, are chipping away at your own magic. Don't discredit the phenomenal human being that you are; you don't deserve that. The rest of the planet doesn't deserve that.

We need ALL of your awesomeness!

Next time you catch yourself making those negative comments, tell yourself: **"Quit talking smack about my best friend [FILL IN YOUR NAME]"**. It also helps to pair this with a positive affirmation.

Cut back to Tammy:

During one of our sessions I asked, "So if your inner critic is your mother, what is she saying in your head, over and over again?"

"'What's the matter with you?' is what I hear it saying all the time," she responded.

"What's a positive affirmation you can turn that into?" I asked.

With missing a beat, she responded:

"There is nothing wrong with me. I am perfect the way I am."

Love yourself by complimenting yourself and telling yourself what a great job you are doing—even if you don't believe it right away. Do this often enough, and you'll start to interrupt old patterns by replacing a bad habit with a good habit.

You'll soon embody the fact don't have to try to be perfect at all, because you already are.

Just be you. You're enough.

CHAPTER FOUR

CUT THIS ONE QUESTION FROM
YOUR VOCABULARY

E VERYONE SEEMS SO BUSY, STRESSED out, overwhelmed, and worried about the future. We're supposed to take time to "smell the flowers", but who has time for that? The kids need to be picked up, dinner needs to be on the table, the boss is calling, you need to work late—and let's not even think about those times when you've gotten laid off from your job, you're having a rough time with family, or any of those dark phases in life when you desperately need to lighten your load.

2011 was that year for me. My marriage had ended, my Mom died of ovarian cancer, and eleven other people in my life died that year. Then I moved 2,000 miles away from my support structure to take a dream job that wound up being a total nightmare. I was lost, felt out of control, and the future looked bleaker than I'd ever thought possible.

To say I was stalled and stressed out was an understatement. When we're in these moments, we know that blaming our circumstances does us no good, but we do it anyway. In our exhaustion, we forget to breathe and see the richness that life has to offer. In doing so, we craft a lovely explanation for why life sucks at the moment, and it is one that leaves us powerless.

You know what I learned in 2011?

Don't get stuck asking yourself the question "Why Me?!".

Asking this question is a natural reaction to what is going on, but don't spend time a lot of time on it. It will get you nowhere. Have it over for dinner, have a few drinks with it, but don't let it sleep in your bed because you will regret it in the morning.

See, going to sleep with "Why Me?" will not only color your waking moments, but it will impact your dreams as well, embedding itself on your brain as a new neuronal pathway. What was merely a question blurted out last night in a fit of rage by an upset five-year-old having a tantrum becomes a part of who you think you really are.

You'll forget it was merely one thought (among many) and it will now become a part of a new reality.

"Why me?" leaves you powerless because by assuming the role of victim, you're holding onto things that aren't serving you instead of letting them go. If you were a monkey in the jungle, this victimhood would seal your fate. How so?

Legend has it that trappers use this unwillingness to let go in order to catch monkeys. First, they cut a hole in a box big enough only for a monkey's arm or a banana, but not both.

Then they put bananas inside the box. A monkey comes along and grabs a banana but can't get both its hand and the banana out of the box. The monkey will stay with its arm inside the box because it won't let go of the banana—sacrificing its own freedom.

The great part is that you now have the tools and perspective to put down the banana. You will survive. Seriously, you will.

It may not seem like it at the time. Life may seem so much bigger than you are, but it isn't. I'm sure you've had at least one other experience in life where it felt like all hell's breaking loose, and that you'd never get over it.

Think about it; take a minute and think back over all the years you have lived and bring one event to mind that seemed completely overwhelming. Got it? Good.

If you survived that part of life, you will survive this one.

But I don't want you to simply survive, I want you to thrive. You can do that be viewing everything that comes your way as moments meant to teach you something. If you ask yourself pondering questions like the ones included in this chapter, this will become a habit.

Be a better you by asking these three questions INSTEAD of "Why Me?":

1. "What could I learn from what is happening in my life right now?"

Answering this will take courage on your part to do some serious self-reflection. It won't be easy, but it will give you far more power in your life. Every successful person, the ones we tend to look to for inspiration in our own lives, has faced their fair share of setbacks before, during, and after achieving something great.

What made them successful was taking the time to examine what was happening in their life and squeezing every possible drop of wisdom from it.

2. What do I resent about what is happening in this situation that I am willing to let go of?

The definition of resentment is "feeling displeasure or indignation at some act, remark, person, etc. regarded as causing injury or insult". Look, maybe someone did intentionally set out to cause you displeasure or indignation— that is for them to deal with.

Don't you give away your power by continuing to be angry at the person or situation. The only person harmed by you holding on to your resentment is you.

3. What did I step over or ignore that led to this circumstance? Where did I compromise my values and give into something I knew wasn't right for me or my life?

This is a big one. Stepping over something is like stepping over the dog poop in your backyard. The more you leave it, the less room your dog has for running around. Stepping over issues in our lives is the same kind of thing.

The more issues you step over, the less freedom you experience to be yourself and express yourself.

Sometimes there is power in taking it easy when things get tough. You may find yourself more effective when you take the time to reflect on what's ACTUALLY happening around you rather than resisting reality. Resistance generally leads to feeling even more stuck and that wastes your energy. This energy you could be spending on solutions.

When you're open to what's happening around you, you can be creative, resourceful, and maybe even fearless.

Life's ridiculousness will never respond to the question "Why Me?", but it will respond without fail to your action and the change you create for yourself.

CHAPTER FIVE

QUIT WISHING YOU DIDN'T FEEL "THIS WAY"

ONE MORNING, AS I TOOK another bite of my toast, my eyes welled up with tears, and my breath caught in my throat. I was feeling particularly overwhelmed and sad this morning because of some things that were happening in my life—nothing huge, just the stuff of life. I sometimes refer to this as "First World Problems".

However, I couldn't dismiss my mood. And it didn't diminish the fact that, right then, I missed my mom terribly. She was always the one I called when I was feeling blue. I just wanted to hear her soft voice say, "Aaaawwww honey, I'm sorry that's going on, I know you'll get through this. It is just hard right now. What can I do to help?" I loved that about her– she usually gave reassurance instead of advice. Since I couldn't call her, I simply allowed myself to cry. I allowed myself to feel the sadness and self-pity I was experiencing. In a few minutes, I felt better.

Yesterday I was talking to a friend who is facing a probable diagnosis of ALS (Amyotrophic Lateral Sclerosis). This guy is a multi-talented, exceptional businessman with an amazing life. I couldn't imagine what it was like to face that diagnosis.

"How are you doing?" I asked. "Well," he said, "I've gone from crying three or four times a day to only crying once a day". Alarm bells went off in my head. "Why is that so important to you?"

I asked. "Well, I don't want to burden my family or friends," he responded.

His response was human—we don't want to feel sad or burden others by our worries. The diagnosis my friend was facing sucks. Whether someone is facing a terminal illness or dealing with any other difficult situation, it is very important to feel and express our emotions. But somewhere along the way, we decide we shouldn't let our feelings get in the way. The way of what? Our humanity?

As the French novelist Jean-Baptiste Alphonse Karr said, "Plus ça change, plus c'est la même chose". Directly translated, this means, "The more it changes, the more it is the same thing." In other words, if you try to make yourself happy when you truly feel happy, the sadness will still be there.

Don't try to "change" how you feel. Breathe into it, and allow yourself to feel your emotions. Before you know it, the feeling will pass.

Experience everything—don't shove it away. Move through your feelings. Don't eat them, ignore them, or bury them away. Sometimes you'll have to do this moment by moment. Just grab those snarling dogs by the ears, and look them straight in their eyes. If you don't deal with your emotions, all of the "what ifs," the "how abouts," the "why nots," will all come up to bite you in the butt down the road.

Now don't get me wrong; you don't have to resign yourself to feeling a feeling until it passes or magically leaves you. When you believe you've gotten to the root of what you're feeling and taken the appropriate time to embrace it, you have every right to take actions to shift your mood to another place.

I find it useful to mentally fill in the sentence: "I will feel better when," but if that doesn't do the trick, try the following to completely and fully shift yourself into a new place:

Eat something nutritious. Fluctuating blood sugar levels can affect your mood and emotions. Do you find yourself angry when you are hungry? Or do you ever become unfocused when you haven't eaten for a while? Often we've simply become accustomed to these moods and don't realize we really need to eat. This is why it is often recommended to eat something every two to three hours, so that you keep your blood sugar levels on an even keel.

Enjoy your favorite scent. Our sense of smell is inherently tied to our olfactory receptors, which have strong input into the amygdala. Our amygdala is the emotional center of our brain and the one that generates that "fight, flight, or freeze" mentality. Essential oils are a great gateway to your limbic system. Unhappy? Try anything citrus—orange, lemon, bergamot to increase your happiness quotient. Feeling stressed? Try lavender or chamomile. Can't concentrate? Try peppermint or cinnamon.

Change your physical environment. A change of venue or position will change your mood. The results of several research studies reveal that rooms with bright light, both natural and artificial, can improve health outcomes including depression, agitation, and sleep. If you can't alter the room you are in, then get yourself out of the room. Get up. Walk around. Flap your arms like a bird. Skip around your office. Do whatever it takes to move energy through your body.

At the very least, it will make you laugh, and laughter is truly the best medicine.

Exercise. We have all heard that exercise increases endorphins. That is the natural runners high people talk about. Increasing endorphins will naturally change your mood from bad to good in a matter of minutes. Regular exercise can have a profoundly positive impact on not only your mood, but your sleep and energy levels as well. You don't have to exercise intensely to make this shift either. Research indicates that modest amounts of exercise can make a difference in mood.

Meditate. Use a 5:2:5 breathing technique that I love. Breathe in for 5 seconds, hold for 2, then breathe out to the count of 5 seconds. Take 10 of these deep breaths. Imagine the word "Peace" appearing on the inside of your forehead. If you don't like that word, use another positive word such as happiness, compassion, forgiveness, kindness, or anything you choose.

Every time you inhale, imagine you are inhaling the affirmation. Each time you exhale, imagine you are exhaling your bad mood.

Feeling my feelings in the moment I am feeling them is one of the most important tools that I use on a daily basis to feel powerful, no matter my circumstances.

What causes our feelings to "get in the way" is when we DON'T let ourselves feel them. Pushing our feelings down only makes them more intense, and causes more disease physically, mentally, emotionally, and spiritually.

When we allow ourselves to feel sad, angry, ashamed, guilty, or whatever we are feeling in the moment, the feeling dissipates and eventually disappears. When that happens, you will find yourself with the wisdom you want and options you never believed were possible.

CHAPTER SIX

PLAY BIG WITHOUT BURNING OUT

L ET'S GO BACK TO 1998 when I was in the second year of operating my consulting company. Not only was I hitting my stride, but I was hitting it out of the park. People were seeking me out, and all the business I had was entirely by word of mouth. I should've been happy, grateful and satisfied. Instead, I was completely overwhelmed and annoyed.

I'm sure you've been there. You know the scenario: You've been in back-to-back meetings all day and your to do list keeps growing. You wonder when you are going to find the time to get your work done, let alone hit the gym and/or spend time with friends/family/ significant other. You've forgotten about your new meditation practice, or your commitment to stop eating out and cook at home, or the book you started a few weeks ago. And planning? Forget about it. You are way too busy putting out fires.

How do you go from being overwhelmed and annoyed to feeling satisfied and grateful, especially in the middle of feeling like a chicken with your head cut off?

People keep talking about "having it all", but that doesn't even seem remotely possible when you're at this point.

Cut back to overwhelmed 1998 me. My phone rang, and a key partner who needed to schedule some time with me was on the other end of the line. The advice she gave me during that call I still use to this day. I am eternally grateful for these precious nuggets of wisdom.

"I understand how much you think you have to do, but how many things do you really have to do?" she asked. "In reality, you have a finite to do list. It may be 100 things, but it is finite. It seems overwhelming because you aren't connected to reality," she finished.

Boy, did she know what she was talking about. I took all the little notes scattered around my desk and put them into one big list. I had exactly sixty-three things to do (funny how those kinds of numbers stick with you). She then recommended I estimate the amount of time each item would take and schedule an appointment for the work to be done in my calendar.

"You can schedule yourself a month, three months or a year out based on your deadlines," she coached.

"The point is to get everything into a real timeframe."

I turned this into a mantra—"Only Deal With Reality" and a three step process that I utilize with my clients who are stuck in that same place I was:

1. Write Everything Down In One Place

If you are like most people, you have post it notes or scribble pads in your house, in your car, and on your computer at work. And if you're like most people, you probably find yourself hunting for that "great idea" that you had last week in your Monday morning meeting, or scrambling to find the address to an appointment you're late to.

Use ONE, and only ONE notebook to do this. I call this a "Reality Notebook." It can be a notebook of any kind, including using your phone or an application like Google Keep to track everything.

The point is to have it all in one place and to have it portable, so that you can bring it from meeting to meeting.

2. Reality Check List

At the end of each day go back through your "Reality Notebook" and find all of your to-do's and put them into a simple Excel spreadsheet. (Again, you also can use Google Tasks or another CRM that includes a place to put all of your to-do's.) I generally divide mine up by category, so some are personal and others have to do with work or community.

You can create as many or as few categories as you'd like, but try to keep it simple. Include a due date for each item and estimate the amount of time it will take.

3. Use Your Calendar

During this same time, look out into your week and schedule the top priority items from your "Reality Checklist" into your calendar. People are great about making and keeping promises to others, but not so great about making and keeping promises to themselves. Schedule appointments with yourself to get your work done; include going to the gym, your weekend chores, personal development, reading, etc. Feel free to schedule things a few weeks out, as long as it is in reality! Now, honor those appointments you just made with yourself.

You know when you're reaching your outer limit. You feel exhausted, irritable, and become a person you don't recognize. The moment you begin to feel this way, revisit your reality checklist and calendar. What should be bumped to a later date? Do you see items that would be better handled by someone on your team or in your circle? Which items should you have said no to in the first place?

Reconnecting responsibilities to the actual time we have in reality is an ongoing process for most of us.

You're only one person, but if you continue to follow these three steps, you will find you have more time than you think!

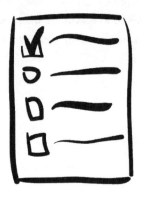

CHAPTER SEVEN

GET ACCOUNTABLE... FOR REAL THIS TIME

THINKING ABOUT BEING HELD ACCOUNTABLE for something probably doesn't make you feel all warm and fuzzy inside. It's rare that we think, "Yay, please ask me, in the middle of a meeting, where that report is that I haven't finished yet. Bring it on!"

Yet, successful people embrace accountability. They find accountability partners that won't let them off the hook and buy their stories or excuses. They find people who will remind them they can achieve whatever they set out to do.

So how why does everyone else feel negatively toward accountability? The very definition of accountability is at the root of the problem. Here is the definition:

"Subject to the obligation to report, explain, or justify something."

The definition begins with the words "subject to." This brings up an automatic "me versus you" phenomenon. The word "obligated" implies you have no choice in the matter. Finally, asking me to defend or justify something automatically puts a person on the defensive. In this ordinary definition, accountability is a threat and you are left feeling powerless.

What if we simply looked at accountability as a contract between two people, whether at work or in your personal life? For example: I give my word (freely) to you to do X, and I give my permission (freely) to you to hold me to account for that. All of this is of my own free will.

This new definition opens new possibilities for accountability. When the threat is taken away, you have the power to hold yourself to account—you don't need anyone else to do so even though you have made the contract with someone else.

Some may argue that it isn't your free will at work if you have to make a promise to your boss. I disagree; you took the job in the first place, knowing full well the job description and what was expected of you.

Even in this scenario, you are acting out of free will and have total choice about the situation.

Here's my other beef with this scenario: Why wait for someone else to call you to task? It is way more powerful to hold yourself to account for your successes as well as your failures. You were the one who made the promise in the first place, and when you go to your boss about an issue instead of the other way around, you are not defending yourself. With this perspective of accountability, you'll find new inspiration for the way you work and how you handle yourself at work.

While you're at it, you can "call one on yourself" by getting to the root of some of the stories you've been telling yourself. These are probably about why things haven't unfolded the way you envisioned—your excuses, your mental dead ends, and your stories.

Doing so requires seeing things as they actually are, limitations and all, and asking hard and careful questions about how they got to be that way.

Try the following:

1. Write down 5 goals/outcomes you want to achieve. (HINT: It's smart to do this work in the same place that you keep and/or map your "Reality Checklist").

2. Rank them in order of importance.

3. Write down the 3-5 excuses you make on a regular basis. Write down the first things that come to mind, even if they make no sense to you. For example: I'm too busy, It's too cold, I don't have X, I was too tired…

4. For each excuse, answer the following questions:

What's the underlying thought or fear? Take a deep breath, pause and notice what thought or feeling pops up. Then whatever it is, write it out below. What's the impact of this excuse? How are your excuses affecting you your life, and your relationship with yourself and others? What opportunities have you missed?

5. What could you say instead? Think about the goal you want to achieve and why. One idea is to acknowledge your fears/feelings and then commit to take one step towards your goal, no matter how small.

6. What will you do with this information? With this knowledge, what steps will you take to address your fear(s), lack of resources, motivation, or self-beliefs?

Ultimately, holding yourself to account is all about building habits to address your fears, lack of resources, motivation and so on. It can be helpful to enlist a partner as you build those habits. Find someone, an accountability partner, to help you obsess about what's going right and help you get in front of blind spots, rather than someone to call you out when you fall short of your goals.

CHAPTER EIGHT

FIND YOUR COMMUNITY, COMRADES, & CONFIDANTS

O VER THE FIVE YEARS I lived with my mom's cancer diagnosis, I became very skilled at creating community. Reaching out to people to tell the truth about how I was feeling and asking for support wasn't easy at first, but it got easier and easier as time went on.

You see, we "independent" people often think we should be able to handle things on our own. We're afraid to open up because we fear we'll be embarrassed by revealing that we don't have it all together. And worse, we're uncomfortable reaching out to others because we don't want to burden anyone else. On the other hand, people love supporting their friends and family in need. We so rarely get to support each other because we're all so busy trying to be brave and not burden each other.

It's all a little nonsensical.

I found that each time I let go of my fears and opened up to someone, it was as if the universe knew to bring me just the right

---

person, who said just the right things at just the right time. It's what I call "Divine Right Timing".

Here's the thing; "Divine Right Timing" can't happen unless you get out of your comfort zone, be vulnerable, and tell someone all of the details of what is really going on with you.

Saying everything is important for two reasons:

1. If you don't say how you are really feeling, your community won't know how to support you. You honestly may not know what you need other than a compassionate ear at that moment, so let them make suggestions and then see what works for you. As you reach out to your community, allow yourself to answer the question, "What am I dealing with right now?", as you share with them.

2. You need to get all of those thoughts out of that space between your ears that have been keeping you up at night. Sometimes we just need a "witness" to our pain and to realize we're not alone.

You'll find that when you say the things out loud that you've been thinking, they often don't feel as dramatic as you've made them out to be, or you'll come up with a solution during the conversation. As you get out all those thoughts, ask yourself, "What would I have to let go of to reach out to someone and share myself?"

Recently, I was reminded again of just how good community is for us. I attended something called the "National Publicity Summit"—a unique, closed-door event where you can listen to top producers, journalists, and editors reveal the secrets of getting coverage in their media outreach, then personally meet with them one-on-one to discuss the possibility of doing a story.

Taking advantage of this unique experience was one of a kind, but not for the reasons you may think of initially. Meeting with representatives of shows like *The View, Good Morning America, 48*

Hours, and others was impressive. However, even more impressive were the attendees. Hearing their stories, their unique gifts, and the contribution and difference they want to make for the world made an indelible impression on me.

There was an interior designer who wants people's homes to reflect their soul and created the phrase "Soulscaping" and wrote a book about it. A successful businessman who lost everything including his father and brother and blamed the world for his circumstances until he mastered personal responsibility, now coaches others to have the courage to face their own fears. A woman who has started a movement to make sure that women operate at their peak performance called "Gutsy Women Win." Those are just a handful of the inspiring people I met. Talk about Divine Right Timing!

By attending this event, I was reminded that I'm just as special as these brilliant people. We all sat around in awe of each other's accomplishments—having your "specialness" reflected back to you is really something!

Having and building your community can help you to not only process and handle things that you just can't manage on your own, but to also see yourself more clearly and be inspired toward more than you might have thought was possible.

But here's the thing—it won't happen unless you get out of your comfort zone.

Getting out of your comfort zone means you'll have to let go of any anxiety you may feel about "revealing" yourself to people.

How do you do that? Let's begin by looking at this word "anxiety."

There is the clinical diagnosis that you may be familiar with, but I'm not talking about that type of severe anxiety.

I'm talking about the sort of ordinary, everyday feelings of anxiousness that we all get from time to time. The kind that might be the result of some stress or uneasiness.

This is the "anxiety" most of us can identify with because it happens anytime we think of doing something new and aren't certain of the outcome. In the physical world that may manifest in sweaty palms, increased heart rate, a queasy feeling in the pit of your stomach.

What if those same feelings weren't caused by distress, but instead were the result of how committed you were to achieving an outcome? When you are on a roller coaster the feeling you get in the pit of your stomach could be fear, but in another scenario, it could also be excitement. Same feeling, different circumstances.

Let's turn those sweaty palms and elevated heart rate into something that would motivate us.

I often invite my clients to give themselves an "Anxiety Colonic". Sounds fun, right? Really, it's a quick exercise you can use to "flush" anxiety away. Here's how to do it:

1. **Write Down What You Are Anxious About:** Get it all down on a piece of paper. Every little bit. Likely what you are anxious about isn't real, and it is the result of some story you are telling yourself.

2. **Highlight the Facts:** Take this step seriously. Use a highlighter and highlight the who, what, where, and when of this anxiety-inducing situation. You will likely find that the facts take up 1% of the page and 99% of the page is filled with our stories. Now that you can see the facts, you can be a bit more objective.

3. **Then Ask Yourself, What Do I Really Want?** What if those feelings aren't feelings of distress, but actually a result of something you are committed to achieving? What do you really want? In my case, it's connecting with new people and building my community.

Jen Coken

4. Then Ask Yourself, Why Do I Want This? In my case, building community and effectively connecting with new people is about feeling less alone in life, and having people around me that help me fulfill my soul's purpose. You'll have your own reasons, and that's perfect.

You see, when we get connected to what we really want, we often see new actions to take to get us there. Recognizing and understanding your anxiety allows you to make powerful choices in the moment. That's how you flush your anxiety away.

Forget the small talk. Instead, reach out to someone and tell them all of the details of what is really going on with you. Build the right community—one that will give you the strength to act on your ideas and inspire you to be the best version of you.

CHAPTER NINE

ASK IF YOU CAN PLAY

PICTURE THIS: IT'S SATURDAY MORNING. I've already been to the gym and I'm walking home from Starbucks with my Venti iced coffee with two inches of soy. (I swear I've tried those ½ caf, ½ decaf, triple-pump-sugar-free caramel-iced-skinny-soy-latte concoctions, but I'm a simple woman with simple tastes.)

Across the street, I see my neighbors hard at work planting what looks to be a community garden. It's a bit chilly, but there they are, in their floppy hats and gardening shoes. One woman is obviously in charge because she is wearing an orange safety vest, just in case an errant squirrel steps on a rack and squashes someone in the nose. She's the type that probably has Band-aids in one of her pockets.

Digging in the dirt and planting looked so much fun that for a brief moment I was transported back to childhood. In fact, the words, "Can I play?" almost came out of my mouth.

I'd never walk up to a group of strangers and ask if I can play. But why is this so difficult now, when it was so easy when we were kids?

Could it be because when we asked if we could play as kids, the answer was "no" one too many times? Maybe over time we learned to be more cautious and careful, sussing out the situation like two wrestlers circling each other, and then only warily testing the waters after the threat seemed manageable.

Or maybe, if you are like me, you get anxious around big groups of new people, whether at a Saturday morning volunteer effort or an after-work networking event. From the outside I seem like a people person, an extrovert (and my Myers Briggs Personality Assessment would agree). But on the inside, I am like squishy.

Jello—feeling a bit unstable, off balance and out of whack.

I know that the anxiety I feel is a defense mechanism I put together when I was a kid. I was 5'9" by the 9th grade, with braces and thick glasses. I had grown so fast I couldn't keep up with my body. I used to trip a lot going up steps (I had size 11 feet when shoes only went to a size 10 at the time). I always felt awkward and out of place. **I still feel that same dread in the pit of my stomach when I approach new people, but I no longer let it stop me.**

Thirty-five years after 9th grade, I've decided the world is our playground. Incredible things open up for each of us if when we see life as an opportunity to play, contribute, and be creative—the trick is finding the grown-up versions of "Can I play?" for yourself.

Me, well, I've had great success with these two variations:

1. "What's new with you THIS WEEK?"

Asking people what's new in the past week gives people a recent experience they can talk about. They don't have to think too hard and check into their memory banks. Instead they can say "Well, I crashed my car yesterday, that was new."

2. "Anything new in your life to celebrate?"

Asking people about things they want to celebrate gives them an opportunity to be in the space of gratitude and happiness.

According to Dr. Marianna Pochelli, N.D., "Thinking positive, happy, hopeful, optimistic, (and) joyful thoughts decreases cortisol and produces serotonin, which creates a sense of well-being".

What a great way to kick things off with a stranger! Lead them to create their own happiness—cool, eh? And remember, before you ask those questions, have your own answers ready, because inevitably the person you are talking to will ask you the same.

You're probably thinking, "These are great, but I'll still have that squishy Jello feeling you mentioned before".

You always will. Just don't let it stop you.

I'd invite you to recognize that your anxiety is not real—it's just a feeling triggered by your memories of rejection. Know that the feeling will pass (just like the gas you feel after eating a big meal).

Once you shift your viewpoint about the situation from "this is going to be really scary" to "I wonder what fascinating person I will meet at this event?", you'll have no problem connecting with new people on the slide, swings, and monkey bars of life.

CHAPTER TEN

KISS PEOPLE PLEASING GOODBYE

B E FOREWARNED, YOU ARE ABOUT to hear some very personal details about my life.

I had a hysterectomy in June of 2014. The night before the surgery, I sent an email out to my family and closest friends who wanted updates. In that I email I shared that I was worried about the surgery. The type of surgery I would have was dependent upon the size of my fibroids and whether the doctors could do a "Laparoscopically Assisted Vaginal Hysterectomy". I didn't want them to have to make an incision (no matter how small) and asked everyone on the email chain to share my intention that the surgery be done laparoscopically.

My cousin, a nurse in the practice responded, "Don't worry Cousin! You are in the hands of a very skilled surgeon. If anyone can remove a load of crap from your vagina, it is her!"

My cousin was right. The doctor was, indeed, able to pull a load of crap from my vagina. My uterus was four times the average size and weighed 851 grams (yeah, you can pick your jaw up off the floor). I felt much better physically after the surgery. Every day, I felt more like myself and the lower back pain I had experienced for months had disappeared. I was surprised by the emotional transformation I experienced—and the new view I acquired.

See, I've always been a people pleaser. I love taking care of other people. But when I was the one that needed to be taken care of, it was hard for me to articulate what I needed and even harder to ask. I've always been a perfectionist. It was always a great motivator when I was on the campaign trail, or creating a new company, or a new project. It doesn't work so well when other people just want to love and care for me in the way they want to show it.

I never saw how much of a straight-jacket this was until I completely lost my temper with a truly great friend that had stopped by to check on me after my surgery. When she finally left, I spent the day thinking about my behavior, what had motivated me, and how that scenario had played out so many times in my life. (Thankfully that truly great friend is also truly gracious. We talked. She forgave me. Then I forgave myself.)

The question I have for you is—what makes YOU happy?

So often we assign happiness (or sadness or madness) to forces outside of ourselves—he/she did it to me, that was unfair, that situation shouldn't have happened. But you have the power to respond to any situation, so even in the worst of times you can choose happiness.

Grab a pen and answer these questions (don't think about it, just write!)

1. What I have learned so far about what happiness is for me? (make a list)

2. What blocks me from feeling happy? (make a list)

3. I take ownership of the following blocks to my happiness (make a list)

Jen Coken

4. I need to let go of, or say "No," to (make a list)

5. I am thankful for (make a list)

When I walked myself through this exercise I decided to make a change in my life, and a big one.

Now, every day around 4:00pm, I sit by my pool in the sunshine every afternoon for an hour kibitzing (that is yiddish for chatting) with my neighbors.

I began to notice how much happier I was after a few days of being in the sun, getting to know my neighbors, and simply relaxing. In the past I never would've taken an hour from 4:00 pm to 5:00 pm to do this, because I was not being "productive". The kicker was that I was way MORE productive after taking that hour for me.

Perfectionism and people pleasing are not always the cause for problems. They become problematic when we are unaware that we are fueled by these habits. When that happens, we become like hamsters on a wheel. We are always trying to get somewhere and never going anywhere, and the things that used to make us happy now feel like obligations.

Take time each day to do one thing that makes your heart sing. Do something that fills you up and makes your toes curl and a giggle escape from you lips. You'll find yourself people pleasing less, articulating what you need on a more frequent basis, and off the wheel. Like a hamster, nestled in shredded newspaper, fat cheeks and all.

CHAPTER ELEVEN

SAY HELL YES!

A RE YOU A "YES" MAN/WOMAN? You know what I mean. That kind of person that says yes when someone asks for a favor, foregoing your needs? That kind of person that says yes because, like me, you are afraid of missing out?

Or maybe, also like me, you say yes when you really mean maybe or even no, because you don't want to hurt someone's feelings. To be fair, sometimes saying yes can cause breakthroughs. I started saying YES to all social activities I was invited to about 20 years ago. I realized, as outgoing as I was, I said NO a lot because I had anxiety about entering a room of people I didn't know. So, I took on saying YES to parties, drinks with new friends, and hikes with groups of strangers.

It had a profound effect on me. My social anxiety disappeared and I no longer felt like a fake when I said, "It's so good to meet you," because now I honestly meant it.

That was a real turning point for me in my life, and I'm glad I did it. However, I also want to get better at setting my own personal boundaries.

The biggest thing that stops me from setting and holding my own personal boundaries is my fear that I will hurt someone's feelings if I say no. If you ask me to help you to move, I say yes to the exact times you need me, yet show up stressed out because I skipped my workout to help you. Then, I feel resentful because I didn't ask for what I really wanted, which was to come after AFTER yoga class. You want to go hear music tonight? Sure. I put on my "game" face and force myself to be social, even though I'd rather be home with a good book. I'm not hearing the music because I'm not present at all, and I go home early because I'm "tired".

So how did I learn to set boundaries in my life? It's still a work in progress. I learned a lot about myself during a two-week trip with two friends in Ireland. We've known each other for over a decade, but never traveled together. We went to celebrate our birthdays, and to scout out the area to lead a woman-only empowerment retreat.

I love these two people and they love me. All three of us are highly trained coaches. We even had a phone call prior to leaving to talk about our expectations, how we liked to travel, and other potential points of conflict. In short, we did everything we could to have a great time, and we did! But traveling together can be challenging no matter how much planning you put into it, how much you like each other, or how well trained you are.

I got sick while on the trip and instead of becoming a martyr or a victim, I chose to take care of myself and stay home a few nights. I also let my friends take care of me, something "Ms. Independent" doesn't always do well. I learned how to take care of my own needs. I developed new ways of communicating so I could say what I wanted. I wasn't always the most eloquent, but I developed some new self-care muscle. My friends were full of compassion and grace, and helped me along the way.

Here are some questions for you to ponder:

Where are you already leading in your own life?

Where have you been avoiding taking ownership of your needs or goals?

What do you need to learn about yourself to leap forwards in your life?

Where are you doing what's convenient, rather than committing to yourself?

Where are you wasting time and not getting started on what really matters?

Sometimes stress can simply be a result of doing things we just don't like doing. This deceptively simple exercise brings clarity to your daily activities, so that you can bring more of what you love and cut out what you loathe in your life.

Over the course of a week or so, make a brief note whenever you are doing something you love to do, or you are doing something you loathe doing. We can't always get out of what we loathe doing, so keeping track will give you some insight and potentially identify a limitation you have about saying no.

The more specific you can be, the better this exercise will serve you. If something comes up several times, put a tally mark or number next to it. Make sure to identify/count each separate instance. At the end of the week, review your notes.

What common threads and patterns do you begin to notice? How could you reduce doing what you loathe or make doing it a little easier or more pleasurable? Better yet, come up with some ideas of things you could do to increase doing what you love.

When your priorities are clear in your mind, it's easy to only agree to things that are a "HELL YES!"

Everything else—skipping your workout, staying out too la'
lugging around heavy boxes on a Saturday—becomes a res<
and easy to utter "HELL NO."

CHAPTER TWELVE

STOP, DROP, & ROLL OUT OF
TOUGH CONVERSATIONS

Remember Thanksgiving of 2016?

In the United States, we'd just been rocked by the presidential election. Many people were on edge and the conversations that took place across pies, stuffing, and cranberry sauce were tense, to say the least. It's safe to say chats with our extended families haven't gotten much easier since then.

Our culture and news are filled with scandal, misconduct, policy change, and acts of violence that seemed designed to keep us divided, but our resulting conversations don't have to result in harsh words or slammed doors.

Show up as your best self (so that you can eat the bird, instead of flipping it), in these moments by using my "Stop, Drop, and Roll" technique:

STOP the Action

When the conversation turns to politics, or any topic that raises tension, excuse yourself from the table and give yourself a time out.

In situations of high stress, fear or distrust, cortisol floods our brain. We stop being able to strategize, build trust, or be compassionate. The amygdala, our instinctive brain takes over. The brain then makes a chemical choice about how to best protect itself—fight, flight, freeze or appease. To avoid those basic responses, stop talking, excuse yourself from the conversation or table, and find a quiet place to breath.

Go the bathroom, say you have to take a phone call, or whatever it takes to remove yourself from the situation. Take ten deep breaths focusing on slow inhales and exhales by inhaling for five counts, holding for two counts and exhaling for five counts. Deep breathing decreases those feelings of anxiety, slows the heart rate down, and reduces your blood pressure.

DROP the Topic

Once you have calmed down, go back to the table and find a way to divert the topic. Truth be told, no one at the table wants to be embroiled in a political discussion, so someone should redirect the conversation anyway.

It could be something simple like, "Did you see the way that the Ravens beat the Browns last week?", or "Did I tell you that Johnnie got an A in math after struggling all year?"

If those don't work, you can be more direct. "You know what? I don't know about you, but the news these days is really stressful for me. What do you think about saving current events for another time? How about each of us go around the table and say what we are thankful for?"

Come to your dinner prepared with five or ten topics you can use to divert the conversation.

Roll On

Like water on a duck's back, put that argument behind you. Those folks around the table are family and friends, and they've been in your life for a long time. Don't take their opinions or arguments personally. Every person has a viewpoint, which they are entitled to it, just like you are entitled to your viewpoint. Yours isn't better than theirs, and theirs isn't better than yours.

Of course, there will be occasions where speaking up or expressing your opinion is necessary. Truth be told, there are times when having tough conversation is a key to your personal growth and will transform your relationship for the better—these are often the conversations we should NOT stop, drop, and roll over.

To move out of this place, ask yourself the following:

What reasons do you have for not talking to the person?

(List them all!)

What conclusions did I come to about myself, the other person or the situation?

What has been the cost of stepping over this situation?

Now it's time to hold up a mirror—What is this person here to teach you about yourself?

From here, craft a gratitude statement, *"I am thankful that [person's name] held up a mirror so I could learn X."*

Conflict in life is inevitable. Whether it's political banter over the holidays, holding someone accountable at work, or even telling the waiter your meal wasn't quite to your liking, how you deal with it can make or break your success (and sanity).

By approaching your conflicts in a healthy manner, you'll be a little happier, and feel more connected and loving to everyone around you. You'll even feel this way towards your pigheaded Uncle Hank and his obnoxious wife Margaret, if you can believe it!

CONCLUSION
MAKE A HUGE INVESTMENT
(HINT: THIS ISN'T ABOUT STOCKS)

WHEN I THINK BACK OVER all things I've accomplished in my life and the setbacks I've overcome, I realize there were only a few years when I didn't have a coach. As a kid, my Mom was my biggest cheerleader. In college and throughout my early career, I surrounded myself with advisors and mentors who I went to on a regular basis for advice and guidance. I always assumed I didn't have all of the answers, and felt that asking others for their input would reveal something I hadn't imagined. My career choices were predicated upon their advice, and I was successful because I took it.

Around the age of 32, I realized all the advice I was getting wasn't doing the job it once had. I was successful, but my experience of success was short-lived, because I was always moving on to the next thing and therefore was never really satisfied with myself.

I had a lot of friendships and was a very social person but felt lonely in a room full of people. I'd been in love a number of times, but all of my peers were getting married, and I wasn't sure that was the road for me or who to talk to about that. I loved my family, but a lot of the time they drove me crazy and I wasn't sure how to be my best when I wasn't "in the mood" to interact with them.

I realized I had a lot of "buts", so I decided it was time to put my proverbial "butt" on the line. That's when I hired my first life coach and have surrounded myself with coaches over the last 20 years. Why? Because I wanted:

- to be asked questions that made me question myself and made me think outside my own box;

- someone who was not only going to be my biggest cheerleader, but also my biggest challenger;

- someone who could watch my performance and my life from a 30,000-foot view and ask me questions until I came to my own conclusions; and

- someone who could unlock the genie in the bottle (spoiler: that genie was me).

All four things are what a life coach does. This may come across as self-indulgent because I am a life coach—I've delivered these results to over 8,000 people for nearly 20 years. But, let me make myself abundantly clear: I'm not saying hire me (we may not be a fit), I'm simply saying hire a life coach.

Success comes from working in partnership with people around you who will encourage/support/harass/cajole and mostly INSPIRE you to achieve your dreams. Unsuccessful people think they should be able to reach their goals on their own.

Successful people know that success isn't a solo adventure. Take for instance, Warren Buffett when asked by The New York Times "What is the #1 investment a person can make?" he responded, "Invest in yourself."

How do you know if you are ready for a life coach? Ask yourself these four questions:

1. **Are you ready to go beyond what you think you are capable of?**

2. **Are you willing to do the work to produce the result you want?**

3. **Do you welcome someone who will hold you to account and be your partner every step of the way until you succeed?**

4. **Are you coachable? That is, are you willing to consider everything your coach is suggesting and out right give him/her the hand?**

If you answered "yes" to ALL four questions, then you are ready to hire a coach. If you are ready to be coached, the next step is to talk to a few coaches and pick the one who is the best fit. What should you look for in a coach?

It's a simple mix of credibility and chemistry. I recommend looking for someone who has A) overcome the challenges you're facing, and B) can prove they've helped others make the same breakthroughs.

Choose someone you can allow yourself to be vulnerable with, someone who you can picture yourself talking to when you're in the middle of making undeniably uncomfortable changes in your life.

Ideally, your coach will be able to read between your words and guide you toward answers you didn't even think to ask for.

With some passion, attention, and resilience, and a sense of humor, you can start living your best life now. You can achieve the things you've always dreamed of, and stress, less.

If you think you are ready and want to talk to me, schedule a call with me by going to https://discoverywithjen.com, or send an email to me at jencoken@gmail.com. To get a FREE copy of my Success Workbook go to https://jencokenfreebie.com.

To get on my mailing list simply text jencoken to 22828. You will be prompted to enter your email. I send out a weekly email giving you tips on how to embrace the ridiculousness of life! Get on my list IF you are ready to be deliriously satisfied with yourself and the things you achieve.

Manufactured by Amazon.ca
Bolton, ON